PURE PASCHA

Separating pagan from pure on Resurrection Sunday

Michael O'Connor

ACKNOWLEDGEMENTS

I thank my family for their patience and supportive encouragement. Mom and Rachel kept the faith and forgave my often-distracted company. My appreciation to Gillian Fraser who edited my original manuscript, adding much needed order and polish, a mammoth task. Cousin Patrick, thank you for your artistic work on the cover image.

My thanks also to the many church leaders who generously made time to add their insights regarding modern practices on Resurrection Sunday. The kindness of the Hellenic Orthodox congregation of Melrose extended to welcoming me at short notice to offer a Christian motif alternative to worshippers during their most Holy services, you took in a stranger, many thanks.

INTRODUCTION

Sacrificing a human baby to a pagan deity is not something that Christians associate with 'Easter fun'. Nor do we imagine that our material well-being can be improved by presenting an offering of agricultural produce to a fertility idol. However, there are subtleties that have crept into our traditions over millennia, which have resulted in many people today tipping their hat to symbols of just such practices. These unwitting people would never dream of endorsing anything but their precious Christian Faith and its sacred values.

How did it happen? It's simple really, traditional symbols that are handed down from one generation to another are well understood when they are first instituted. Successive generations may be told the significance of these traditional acts and symbols, but like many stories, these explanations become retold with less accuracy and frequency, until the original significance is lost to the mists of time.

I would like to set out the historical origins of the symbols typically used during the Christian Passover, as best I can put the pieces together from old writings and traditions. The purpose here is to inform and not to preach. We live in the information age, and any reader has any number of historical sources available at their fingertips to flesh out this topic. I have by no means attempted to put forward an academic work, there are more studied minds than mine who can do a much better job at that. I have instead put together an overview of the beginnings of the Pagan Easter, as well as the Jewish and Christian Passover, and how these festivals and observances have become intertwined and overlapped during the millennia since their inception. So lower those gun barrels, moms and dads, I'm not here to ruin your children's holiday fun, but only to inform. You can then decide what you want to do with the information.

The Resurrection of Christ after the crucifixion is the central Truth on which the entire Christian Faith is based. It is the lynchpin on which our hope for our own resurrection from physical death depends. I believe that the annual remembrance and observation of this event deserves our whole-hearted participation and clear-minded thought.

Pure Pascha

Publisher: Self

Copyright 2020

First Edition 2021

ISBN: 978-0-620-97182-9

The author has made every effort to obtain permission for and
acknowledge the use of copyrighted material.
Refer all enquiries to the author.
pure.pascha@gmail.com

Views reflected in this publication are not necessarily those of the
publisher, nor the printer.

CONTENTS

CHAPTER 1

THE ORIGINS OF EASTER

The events marking the beginning of the Pagan festival of Easter happened so long ago that different versions of the story abound. What is astounding to a modern researcher are the similarities to be found between the legends in diverse and separate ancient civilisations. The story can be patched together from ancient manuscripts, or from references to those which have been destroyed over time. The Bible and Mesopotamian histories intersect to give us the basic narrative.

In telling the story, I would like to bring you a composite of the versions out there, which will only be comprehensive and detailed enough for our purpose here.

In the biblical book of Genesis, chapters 6-11 record the Great Flood that drowned every land animal except for Noah and his family, after which the family descending from Noah repopulated the earth. One of Noah's three sons was named Ham. Ham had a grandson through his son Cush, named Nimrod. Nimrod is described as being a hunter and a mighty one. This mightiness is further described when it is recorded that Nimrod was a king, and that the beginnings of his kingdom was Babel, later Babylon, which grew to include other regions and towns, notably Assyria and the town of Nineveh.

Modern day geography puts his kingdom roughly in the region between Northern Syria and Iraq, although in later years those regions were to be more closely associated with the descendants of Noah's middle son, Shem. The descendants of Noah's oldest son, Ham, are more closely associated with regions of North Africa, such as Egypt and Libya.

This king Nimrod re-introduced idolatry and occultic mysteries into practice on earth. Historically, most occultic and Pagan practices are traceable to Babel, or Babylon, the Chaldean region. Nimrod had a wife named Semiramis. As a royal couple, they were revered as deities, and no honour was afforded to the God of Noah. Ancient legend from the region tells that when Nimrod died, his body was cut to pieces and scattered far and wide. Semiramis then had the pieces collected, finding all except his reproductive organs. She compensated for this by building phallic structures to symbolise the missing pieces of his body.

After the death of Nimrod, Semiramis was found to be pregnant. The explanation put forward was that Nimrod, now being a heavenly sun-god, had impregnated Semiramis by means of a sunbeam. When Semiramis gave birth to a son, born around the 25th December, the boy was called Tamuz, also recorded as Damuzi, and in other cultures known as Osiris or Adonis. He was proclaimed as the earthly representation of his father, the sun god Nimrod. At 40 years of age, Tamuz was gored to death by a wild boar.

This chain of events in the royal family was prevented from being calamitous by some shrewd story spinning by the powers of the day, chiefly the legend of the mystic egg of Babylon. Supported by the occultic priests and druids of the day, they consolidated the worship of the royal family by establishing the legend that Semiramis had descended from above in a giant egg. The egg landed in the Euphrates River and was rolled to the bank by fish, where doves brooded over it until it hatched. Out of this egg appeared Venus, called Ashtarte.

This new arrival from the sky was Semiramis, who also had the ability to transform a rabbit into an egg-laying bunny in order to convince the rapt earth dwellers of her divinity. So the ancient family was complete, Nimrod as the sun god, Semiramis as the fertility goddess, and their tragically lost son Tamuz. Thus began the Northern hemisphere springtime Pagan fertility festivals. In fact, Pagan fertility practices and ancient occultic practices can be traced in general to the kingdom Babel, as well as Chaldean practices and beliefs.

Many of the civilisations from the Levant will have legends and histories that echo or parallel the story above. Names change from region to region, as can be expected considering the various languages and people groups through which the information was to pass. The lawyer turned historian and academic, Wilhelm Von Bode, wrote about *Estur monap*, or Easter month. Clay tablets originating from Iraq contain the story of a Babylonian Ishtar, the details set out in cuneiform – a system of writing used in the ancient Middle East. Sumerian legend equates the descent of Inanna to Venus as the queen of heaven.

Nimrod was called Bel by the Babylonians, and Semiramis, his wife, was known as Beltis. Other recorded names for Nimrod are Baal, Molech, Moloch, and Baccus. Always referred to as a great hunter, he is revered as the sun god. Semiramis was known as the queen of heaven, Isis in Egypt, Astarte in Caanan, Venus by the Chaldeans, Diana in Ephesus, Ishtar by the Assyrians, Oster in old German, and Istar in Aramaic. The etymology of the English word Easter is easily traceable from earlier names like Ishtar and Istar. Old Pagan references refer to her as the great mother goddess.

The annual Pagan Easter festival started with 40 days of mourning over the death and loss of Tamuz. People were supposed to openly weep and deny themselves of luxuries, often fasting and avoiding alcohol. This 40-day-fast was ended with a sunrise observance after the vernal equinox, overseen by the Pagan priests, and also by a riotous time of drunken orgies in a general free for all, where excess and wantonness was encouraged. The priests impregnated virgins on an altar, and three-month-old babies, conceived during the previous years' proceedings, were killed as sacrifices.

The people traditionally made special foods that served as reminders of the divine royal family. These included cakes baked in the shape of the sun, in worship of the sun god Nimrod, by any name, and for Semiramis, in her capacity as their fertility goddess and queen of heaven. The baked goods and other foods became important symbols to these Pagan ancients, carried forward from generation to generation, and taken with them as they migrated and settled into new areas of the world.

The breads baked to Semiramis were called *bouns*, the origin of the modern term buns. These were eventually assimilated into the early Church, with a cross placed over the top, and became the hot cross buns we know today. We will discover more on that later!

Other traditions were to roast a pig, or ham, remembering the wild boar that had killed Tamuz.

The rabbit (egg-laying bunny) was also replicated in foods. The rabbit is a well-known example of fertility. The purpose and activities of the playboy mansion might spring to mind.

Eggs were and still are used extensively as a reminder of the giant egg that bore Venus, or the fertility goddess, to earth. Druids wore coloured eggs as a symbol of their druidic order. Egg colouring, as part of tradition and festival, has occurred historically in several countries including Egypt, Persia, Japan, China, and across the regions populated by people following the Hindu religion. These were usually brightly painted, often in red, sometimes displayed ornamentally, and exchanged as gifts.

Another symbol associated with the fertility goddess is the pomegranate, with its multitude of seeds representing fertility and production for earth. There are images used depicting the fertility goddess holding a full pomegranate in her hand.

The early origins of the modern symbols of Easter are easily recognised when the ancient symbols are assessed. Humans are creatures of habit, and additionally much storytelling and the passing on of traditions was achieved using pictures, common objects, and symbols. The widespread literacy of today was certainly not commonplace amongst the general population of the civilisations of the regions under discussion.

The use of these symbols and traditions gradually spread into an area from Persia, through the Middle East, up to Mesopotamia, through the Caucuses and eastward into the sub-continent, and from Babylon into the Aegean region, further to Europe, and across the channel into the British Isles. It was to people holding fast these traditions whom the early missionaries and evangelists of the Christian Faith took the Gospel of Christ.

CHAPTER 2

THE ORIGINS OF PASSOVER

The observance and celebration of Passover began as a result of momentous events experienced by a distinct people group, which was pivotal in their emancipation from slavery in Egypt.

As mentioned in Chapter 1 in our study into the history of Easter, we once again refer to the first book of the Bible for record. In Genesis 11:27-36, we read about the family and descendants of Noah's second born son named Shem, beginning with a man named Terah. Terah first lived among the Chaldeans, the site of the early spread of the Easter Paganism (dealt with in the previous chapter). Terah moved his family to live in the land of Canaan, closer to the present state of Israel. Terah had a son named Abram. The chapters of Genesis mentioned above deal with how the God of the Bible established a friendship, communication, and covenant – or oath – with Abram, changing the man's name to Abraham.

The recorded chain of events, including the biological family tree from Abraham forward, is important. We read how God purposed and promised that through this covenant being established with Abraham and his descendants, He would not only set apart a chosen nation, but also bless the world through this nation. God promised to send a Redeemer to save mankind from his separation from God, caused by Adam and Eve's giving in to temptation in the Garden of Eden.

The story continues that Abraham and his wife Sarai, later named Sarah, were childless. A divinely promised son was eventually born to them, named Isaac. A short interlude here must include mention that God had asked Abraham to sacrifice Isaac on an altar. Abraham set off in obedience to this request, with an angel calling him to stop at the moment that Isaac was bound on a stone altar, with the knife in Abraham's hand held aloft for the death strike. God revealed a ram caught in a thicket, which was used as the sacrifice instead, becoming a substitute until God would provide a permanent sacrifice later in history. This willingness on the part of Abraham to obey God and sacrifice his promised son made it possible, centuries later, for God to go through with the sacrifice of His own Son.

The Passover, established between God and the descendants of Abraham and Isaac, contains a type and foreshadowing of this exchange of sacrificial offering.

Moving on down the family line, Abraham's son Isaac, in turn, had twin sons Esau and Jacob. Esau, the first born, sold his birth right to his younger brother Jacob in return for a meal of broth. Jacob then became the brother destined to continue the family name and fortune.

Further events are recorded in Genesis chapters 37-50. Jacob had 12 sons, the second youngest of whom was Joseph (with the multi-coloured coat). As their father's clear favourite son and a dreamer of greatness, Joseph was despised by his siblings. They sold him into slavery to travelling traders, who took him to Egypt and sold him onwards there. Joseph went from managing a household to prison, and from prison to the king's palace as a food storage planner – rising to prime ministerial prominence due to his God-gifted wisdom and foresight. At last his dreams were having a positive effect.

Through storing up harvests and forward planning, Egypt became well-stocked with grain, and consequently held strong leverage in supply negotiations with its neighbours and visitors fleeing the widespread seven-year-drought and famine, which followed seven years of bumper harvests. These forced migrants included Joseph's brothers, who had been sent south to Egypt by their father, Jacob, in order to buy food for their survival. At first they did not recognise Joseph as their brother, however, after a fair number of tactical ploys and manoeuvring on Joseph's part, his identity was revealed, and the family group numbering 70 moved to settle in Egypt.

The sons of Jacob, later renamed Israel, settled in an area called Goshen. They had great success in their work, became wealthy, and grew in population. Their customs and heritage kept their community distinct from the general population of Egypt, and thus they remained a recognisable sub-section.

Many years later, a king ascended to the throne of Egypt who did not have any remembrance of the historical significance that Joseph had to the wealth of the Pharaoh. This new Pharaoh became concerned at the numbers and strength with which the community at Goshen was developing, viewing their strength as a possible danger to the Egyptians in case of an attack from outside the country's borders. Their patriotism was doubted.

A populist decision on the part of Pharaoh was to burden the descendants of Israel with onerous labour and production requirements in service to the country. They were tasked with ever-increasing building targets, and eventually also with supplying the raw materials for building. When these hardships produced the opposite effect to the desired weakening and decimation of numbers, the midwives were instructed to kill all male children at birth. This command was not obeyed by the midwives, to their eternal credit, and the Israelites grew stronger despite imposed hardships.

One of the midwives smuggled a baby boy, who was intended to be murdered, away from harm. He was found and raised in Pharaoh's household. This boy was Moses. A strong sense of community remained in Moses' conscience, and he was forced into exile after killing an Egyptian who was mistreating a Hebrew man. Moses was to return to Egypt after 40 years, guided by the God of Abraham.

After protracted negotiations with Pharaoh, including heaven-sent plagues devastating the entire country – the effects of which were notably absent from Goshen – permission was granted to Moses to lead his people out into the desert to worship God. The last plague was the overnight death of the firstborn sons of every Egyptian, man and beast. This included everyone who was not protected by the display of the blood of a lamb painted over the doorway of their home. Instructions were given to the people to sacrifice a spotless lamb without deformity, to eat the meat in a special meal, and to remain indoors during the night. Information had been given out to the Hebrews that the angel of death would pass over their home if the blood was displayed on the doorposts and lintels. Any spot on the skin or wool of a lamb would represent sin, or a physical blemish would represent a spiritual blemish. The lamb would have to be without spot or blemish, representing a state of sinlessness, in order to qualify the blood on the doorposts as acceptable for the angel of death to pass over the houses.

Remembrance of this event became the foundation of Passover in the Jewish calendar, and of the later death and resurrection of Jesus in the Christian calendar – where Christ is referred to as the Lamb of God who takes away the sin of the world.

Moses inspired and led the descendants of Israel out of Egypt, with the miraculous destruction by drowning of the pursuing Egyptian army, Pharaoh perishing along with his soldiers. Years of wandering the Sinai desert became the formative time of the nation and laws of the Jewish Israel.

When the Mosaic laws were being set out for this newly liberated group, the Passover observance was included as a high holy day, an annual occasion of great significance. The set date was the 14th day of the Jewish calendar month of Nissan. This meant that it occurred on a different day of the week as the years unfolded, and that the days of observance changed each year compared to contemporaneous and later calendars, such as the Julian and Gregorian. The Bible book of Leviticus chapter 23 provides interested readers with details of the establishment of this priestly and community responsibility.

The changing weekday of the Passover, and its disconnect from the Pagan calendar, was to be a point for raging debate and bitter disagreement in the Christian Church just a couple of centuries into its existence. We will study more on that twist in a later chapter covering the Paschal celebrations and observance of the early Church versus the Pagan Easter.

Included with the instruction to observe Passover annually was a warning of what was to be explicitly excluded. The Israelites were told which annual holy days to observe, and that the days were observed in honour of God. They were now moving from Egypt towards a geographic area steeped in the Pagan occultic practices (described in the previous chapter). In Deuteronomy 12:29-32, God warns the people that when they expel other nations out of their Promised Land, they were not to allow curiosity to get the better of them.

This led to the adoption of Pagan worship practices, even if misguidedly directed at worshipping God in some way. The very term *Babel* means confusion and mix-ups, which was the gist of the obtained warning. In verse 31 God, through Moses, mentions that the heathen in the land ahead of them practiced abominations such as burning their sons and daughters in the fire to their gods (this we have already mentioned in discussing the Pagan fertility festival during Easter).

The general rule was that the new pattern of worship given to the Jewish nation was comprehensive and should not be added to nor taken away from. Detailed instructions in Deuteronomy 18:9-14 list many forms of occult practices and divination being practiced by the heathen in Canaan, including child sacrifice, with the important note that the people were to be removed from the land for that very reason. One would have hoped that witnessing this removal of nations from their historic homelands would sear the vital importance of obedience to the command to avoid Pagan practices for their own good into the Israelite community. However, we will see that later generations of Jewish Israelites disregarded the warnings, taking up these practices described as abominations, and were themselves removed from their homeland – going into exile to Babylon, the very seat of the Paganism they embraced.

Once settled in the Promised Land, the people followed a cyclic pattern of worship. Periods of true worship towards God carried on as laid out in the Mosaic Law. Obeying the Passover and other observances and laws saw the nation of Israel prosperous and victorious in the tribal clashes typical of society at the time.

Prosperity led to comfort, comfort to complacency, and the self-willed disobedience to their own laws. Delving into Pagan practices resulted in defeats to their neighbouring enemies, and the nation of Israel was forced to pay tribute and taxes to foreign kings. Leaders, known then as Judges, would be elevated to positions of prominence and civic authority, who would then lead the nation to repent of their waywardness and back to their God. This would bring the people through a time of successful struggle against foreign oppression, leading to freedom and independence once again. This is the national cycle of all people and ages.

These foreign Pagan practices are detailed in the book of Judges 10:6. The names given include the ones with which we are now familiar. Notably Baal and Ashtoreth, gods of Syria, Sidon, Moab, Ammon, and of the Philistines. We know Baal is synonymous with Nimrod and the Pagan fertility practices following his rule. Ashtoreth is the goddess Eostre, queen of heaven to the sun worshippers.

We later see in their history, when Israel was under kings instead of judges, that the conduct of the king very much steered the course for the nation, with the all too familiar consequences. King Solomon married a number of foreign wives – in contravention of the Mosaic Law. These wives led him astray in his old age, introducing Pagan worship to the royal household, displacing the worship of God that is clearly laid out in Mosaic law. Humans are stubborn beings, if nothing else.

Jeremiah was a prophet in the time of the kingdom of Israel. He wrote in the book Jeremiah 7:17-18 that the Israelite families of his day were preparing dough to bake cakes for the queen of heaven. These were not neighbouring nations, but the inhabitants of Judah in Jerusalem. This queen of heaven was Semiramis, consort of Nimrod. In telling of these doings, Jeremiah adds that these actions would provoke anger in the Lord, the God of Israel.

It wasn't as if the relative merits of following God versus Baal were up for debate. A famous story in the time of the kingdom in Israel is that of the prophet Elijah challenging and destroying the rival prophets of Baal in his day. He set them a challenge, in full view of the nation, to determine whose God was real. The idea was to build two stone altars, put a bull carcass on top of a stack of wood on each altar, and not light fire to the wood stacks, but call on their respective gods to burn the offering. The prophets of Baal accepted this challenge and set about calling on Baal to burn the wood and offering. All this was to no avail. At the end of a day of calling for fire, the wood remained as it had begun. Elijah then made a public spectacle of teasing the idol worshippers and their god, following which he doused his offering and woodpile with water. When he called on God to prove Himself, fire came down and completely burnt the meat, wood, and the stones of the altar, and evaporated the water. This dramatic display convinced the people, who had witnessed the event, which deity was more powerful. Elijah immediately instructed the gathered crowd, who had renewed their allegiance to God, to capture every one of those Pagan prophets, and he executed all of them on that day. The subject was a serious one for those committed to being true to God.

Another prophet of the Old Testament was Ezekiel. He writes of an admonishment from God regarding the Pagan practices continued by the Jewish people. In the Bible book of Ezekiel 8:13-18, we read how Ezekiel sees an unfolding vision depicting idol worship in the temple of Jerusalem. The images and paintings displayed in and around peoples' homes were of unclean creatures. Women seated at the north gate of the Jerusalem temple were weeping for Tamuz, participating in the mourning period leading up to the fertility festival held in honour of Semiramis. The vision also included the image of men turning their backs on the temple and worshipping the sun towards the East. Knowing what we know by now, it becomes clear that Pagan worship of the sun god and the queen of heaven was being practiced by God's chosen race in the very temple meant to be holy to Him.

The consequences were even more dire for the people of Judah after this extremely disrespectful and sacrilegious behaviour. The whole nation spent 70 years, a generational lifetime, in captivity, with widespread destruction wreaked on the kingdom by hostile neighbouring people.

The ancient establishment of blessings on obedience, juxtaposed by curses on disobedience, continued unabated as plainly put forth in the Mosaic Law for all to read and know beforehand. Freedom of choice is based on having free will, but once a choice is acted upon, consequence follows that chosen path.

CHAPTER 3

THE LAST LAMB

The foreshadowing of Christ's death on the Cross, that is, the sacrificial lamb offered at Passover according to Mosaic Law, was repeated annually. This changed for the New Testament Christians, who believed in Christ as the Messiah. In the Bible book addressed to the Hebrews, the writer states that Jesus was sacrificed once for all (10:10-12). The one-time sacrifice was enough and the saving grace is available for all mankind from then on. While Jesus Himself said that He came as Messiah for the Jews first, salvation by faith is also extended to the gentiles at large. Anyone who accepts the Lordship and grace made available to them by the sacrifice and resurrection of Jesus as Christ is spiritually grafted into the family of God.

The blood covenant between God and mankind, which had its purpose as the removal of the barrier of sin separating the two, is a two-way agreement, put forward by God, requiring acceptance by a free-willed man or woman.

There are many parallels between the Passover Lamb and the crucifixion of Christ. There are many resources available for those who wish to study the astounding list of overlap between prophecies recorded in the Jewish scriptures, foretelling details of the promised Messiah, and the life story of Jesus, as written and preserved in the Bible Gospels, and also in secular recorded history of the time. Among these are that Jesus' legs were not broken on the Cross, a means used to hasten the death by asphyxiation of the victim, but He was speared in His side, fulfilling prophecy in the Jewish scriptures. This corresponds to the law stating that the original Passover lamb was not allowed to have any blemish or deformity.

Eerily do the words of Pontius Pilate remind us of this concept when he says that he found no fault in Jesus. The timing of His death on the Cross also coincided with the slaughter of the sacrificial lamb in the temple of Jerusalem, only a few kilometres away. Many see a blood-stained cross not only in the actual wooden Cross of crucifixion, but also when drawn from the lintel above the doors in Egypt, from the drainage sill below the door where the blood collected, and then across the doorway from one doorpost to the other. Jesus had that same cross of blood from His head, bloodied by the crown of thorns forced onto it, to His feet and across between His hands, all pierced to keep Him on the Cross of sacrifice.

Also noteworthy was that the lamb could only be slain in Jerusalem, which is where the crucifixion of Christ took place. The Jewish Pesach observance includes three pieces of unleavened bread, the middle of which is broken, hidden, sought, and found during the course of the Passover meal. The parallel seen by some is that the second person of the Triune God, being Jesus the Son, is represented by that middle matzo. He is broken, dies, is buried, and re-appears to mankind after His resurrection. This brings up the pivotal point on which the Christian Faith depends.

The truth of the resurrection is foundational for the Christian Faith, as on it rests the claim of Jesus to be the long-promised Messiah. Many times during His life Jesus told the disciples that He would be handed over to the Sanhedrin, be scourged and crucified, die and be buried, and then be resurrected and appear to them again. These were hefty predictions, and so the historicity of an actual resurrection gives great credence to the trustworthiness of Christ.

Many noble and spiritual individuals have led religions and/ or cultish movements at various times throughout history. Some have even died as an expression of, or defending, their movement. Shrines over the graves of spiritual leaders can be found across the earth. There are none who foretold during their life that they would be willingly put to death as a result of love for people, in order to remove their separating sin, and then return from the dead, accompanied by numerous proofs. None barring Jesus, that is. While there are far more scholarly and voluminous writings on the death and resurrection of Christ, it is necessary to take a careful look at the reasons that make the resurrection believable, which would be proof in turn of Christ's divinity, and that back up His claim to Messiahship.

That Jesus was crucified is not widely argued against in academic circles. All four gospels, the first four books of the New Testament, describe how Jesus was betrayed to the authorities and crucified. His sentencing and means of execution are listed in both Christian, Judaic, and secular writings.

Off the bat, let us be assured that after being whipped to ribbons, being forced to drag a wooden cross out of town, spending hours straining against limbs anchored by nails to a cross in order to escape asphyxiation, and having a Roman soldier thrust his spear into His chest from below His ribcage, Jesus died. A Roman whip, or flagrum, was similar to a cat o' nine tails, with multiple striking ends bearing metal and bone attachments. The Roman legions were legendary in their ability to execute by crucifixion and other means. Death during crucifixion was caused by a combination of blood loss, shock, dehydration, congestive heart failure, and asphyxiation.

The accounts of His death also include mention that a Roman soldier thrust his spear into Jesus' side, instead of the more commonly employed tactic of breaking His legs to accelerate asphyxiation. The spear thrust from below would have pierced His heart and lungs, which in itself is enough to end a life. Any Roman soldier who allowed a condemned prisoner under his charge to escape would face dire consequences, including death. Secular historical sources, including Tacitus, Josephus, Mara Bar-Serapion, and the Jewish Talmud and Toledoth Jesu, all repeat that Jesus died. As already mentioned, Jesus' death is not disputed in serious academic circles.

Conspiracy theorists put forward the idea that Jesus merely swooned on the Cross, but revived after burial. In order for Jesus to be around for the later eyewitness reports of His walk to Emmaus from Jerusalem, a distance of 11 kilometres, He would have had to survive the flogging, crucifixion, and spearing, rolled the heavy gravestone away from the tomb exit, overpowered or evaded the guards who had been set to keep His body buried, and made the return walk in order to be back in the upper room in Jerusalem by the evening. *Not likely*.

Another poor theory is that the women and disciples went to the wrong tomb when going to embalm Jesus' body. Once again, enemies of the Christian Faith abounded who would have loved to point out the correct tomb and the body of Jesus. But they couldn't, because it wasn't there. Too many people knew the location of the tomb of Christ for this theory to hold water. The same women who saw Jesus' body being buried were there on the Sunday morning to embalm the body. They knew the tomb. Peter and John also went to the tomb later that morning. Surely they couldn't all have hurried to the wrong address?

Because Jesus surely died, if He was seen in bodily form afterwards, this adds proof to the resurrection. We have four gospel accounts in the Bible that all include an account of Jesus being seen by first Mary of Magdalene and other women, and then by disciples, family members, and large groups of followers. The apostles passed on not only written witness accounts of having seen Jesus resurrected, but also instances of the prevalent oral tradition of the day. Many early Church fathers would have known the apostles personally and would have received instruction in the faith from them directly. This oral tradition from the apostles was included over time into scripture and church writings. Importantly, many of the apostles and early Christians went to their death by torturous martyrdom for the very confession that Jesus was alive and the Messiah. A well concocted lie would have unravelled under the duress of the stones, the fire, the sword, and the cross with which they were cruelly executed. However, not one apostle or disciple turned at the point of death, all are recorded as accepting suffering and death when given an ultimatum.

These preachers of a risen Jesus and willing sufferers include James, Jesus' half-brother, who was initially a sceptic. Also included was Saul of Tarsus who enters the stage executing Christians and had a meeting with Jesus while journeying to do more of the same. He becomes Saint Paul, a prolific evangelist and writer of much of the New Testament.

So, we see that apostles, disciples, followers, sceptics like half-brother James, and even outspoken enemies like Saul of Tarsus all reported seeing Jesus alive after His execution and burial.

The disciples were executed for their confession of Christ by diverse peoples and authorities of the day. Peter was crucified upside down in Rome, and the same fate of crucifixion awaited Simon the Zealot. Phillip was believed to be martyred in the ancient Greek city of Hierapolis, where he was impaled by iron hooks and hanged upside to die. Andrew was crucified in Greece. After being whipped severely, they tied his body to a cross. He continued to preach to his tormentors for two days until he expired. Judas (Thaddeus) was martyred in Persia on his missionary journey where he was hewed with an axe by religious leaders (Magi). James the Just, the leader of the church in Jerusalem, was thrown off the Temple wall when he refused to deny his faith. Having survived, his enemies killed him with a club. Matthias, who was chosen to replace Judas Iscariot, worked amongst cannibals. Records of his death vary, some record stoning / beheading / crucifixion. Bartholomew, also known as Nathaniel, was a missionary to Asia and present day Turkey. He was martyred in Armenia where he was flayed to death by a whip. Mark, the founder of the church of Alexandria, died in Alexandria after being dragged by horses through the streets. Thomas, of the doubting Thomas fame, was stabbed with spears in India during one of his missionary trips where he established the Church in the sub-continent.

All these apostles and disciples kept their confession steadfast through life and death, they evidently believed what they preached. They held fast to their confession of having seen Jesus alive after the crucifixion and burial.

These eyewitness reports, for which many were killed, were brought out so close to the time and place of the events to which they refer that the risk of the reports being an unverifiable legend is prevented. People living at the time could easily have countered the story. Other writings in contradiction of the gospel accounts were only published many centuries later.

The Qur'an states that Jesus Himself was not crucified, but this was written 600 years after the events took place. The so-called gospel of Barnabas posits that Judas Iscariot didn't commit suicide, but instead went to Jesus while the latter was in prison, and God changed Judas to look like Jesus and then spirited Jesus up to heaven, leaving Judas to be crucified instead. This was written a millennium after Christ and fails to address the standing minimum facts supported by even non-Christian historians. It boils down to a fanciful tale from the middle ages.

The enemies of Christ put forward arguments against the resurrection, but they all struggle for substance against the facts; the empty tomb being a huge problem for doubters. Any time the enemies of the Christian Faith could produce the body of Jesus, they would have been able to disprove claims of His resurrection. Their motivation would have been high to do so, and yet they couldn't, because the tomb was empty.

When the next step was to claim that the body was stolen, the persistent eyewitness reports by friend, sceptic, and enemy alike of having seen Jesus alive, and their willingness without exception to go through torture and martyrdom instead of denying this claim, was strong proof of the verity of their claims. Men do not easily give up their livelihoods, travel on evangelical missionary trips, suffer deprivations, rejection, imprisonment, torture, and execution for what they know is a lie. The authorities of the day also admitted that the grave was empty when they sought to claim a stolen body.

On the eve of His crucifixion, Jesus and His disciples held the traditional Passover meal, which was celebrated and commemorated by His Jewish community. On several occasions leading up to this night, Jesus had told the disciples of the fate awaiting Him, with increasing clarity as the day grew nearer. The disciples were incredulous at first, and eventually even tried to prevent Jesus' perceived acceptance of the very idea. Their perception of His Kingdom was still of an earthly political country, and an end to the yoke of Roman occupation. The full spiritual overthrow of evil, and the eternal victory over the devil, sin, death, the grave, and hell was not understood until afterwards.

During the last Passover meal that Jesus shared with His disciples, He very plainly equated His blood and body with the elements of the meal set before them. This, in turn, represented the blood and flesh of the Passover sacrifice which had saved those behind the display of blood over their doors from the angel of death. He told them very plainly that they were to eat and drink the bread and wine associated with the Passover commemoration, and when doing so to remember Him. The Apostle Paul says in 1 Corinthians 11:26 that when we do this, we proclaim the Lord's death until He comes. This death was different to any other though, even of those who have died in selfless sacrifice for others. Remembrance days for fallen citizens are observed around the world, these pay tribute to the selfless deeds of heroes named and unnamed. The difference at Passover is that we know that within three days we will be celebrating the resurrection of Christ.

Future Passovers were supposed to be a remembrance – not only of the escape from death in Egypt, but also of the escape from eternal spiritual death made available by Christ's self-sacrifice at the Cross of Calvary. This was the understanding of the first apostles and disciples, not least of whom was the Apostle Paul, who described himself as a Pharisee of Pharisees, grounded and taught as he was from youth in the scriptures and doctrine of the Jewish Faith. He who, as the rabbi Saul, had persecuted the early Christian Church to the point of having their followers stoned to death for blasphemy and who was now the doctrinal teacher of the Christian Faith. It was under the leadership and guidance of Saint Paul, and also of the close original disciples of Christ, who obeyed the Lord's instruction to observe the Lord's Supper from the first instance, that the early faithful established the Christ-centred essence of Pascha.

Traditions and observances were to change dramatically with the passage of time. In the beginning of the Christian era, the broad majority of adherents and believers were Jewish, born and raised. This background helped in some ways to foster a unity of purpose and understanding among the early evangelists and teachers of doctrine.

Afterwards, people came to faith in Jesus as Christ from disparate regions, first of the Levant and later from the eastern Mediterranean regions of Europe and Africa, bringing their own life experiences and traditions into the mix. This set the scene for tumultuous events and friction during the formative centuries of communal Christianity.

CHAPTER 4

PASCHA IN THE EARLY CHURCH

L et us say, for ease of reference, that the Christian age began after the resurrection of Christ. Where sins from beforehand were covered by the blood of animal sacrifices, the New Testament is based on the Blood of Christ crucified – which forever atones for the separating sin of man. We turn our attention now to what the first Christians and the early Church made of Passover.

Our earliest clues seem to suggest little change to the observances during Passover, when considering reports of the first apostles and believers. An important event did change the way Jewish observance of Passover could be followed. The temple in Jerusalem was destroyed in AD 70 by the Roman forces, first under General Vespasian – who was proclaimed Roman Emperor in AD 69. General Titus assumed military command and continued the siege of Jerusalem and the resultant destruction of the second temple, as well as the massacre of a number of Zealot revolutionaries and residents of the city. From that time onwards there was no altar on which to officially offer the sacrificial lamb for Passover, resulting in the gradual emergence of substitute elements appearing in the Jewish Passover rites.

The apostles and disciples of Christ, along with new, mostly Jewish believers, were under the doctrinal instruction of knowledgeable leaders such as Saint Paul the Apostle, previously known as Saul of Tarsus, who persecuted the Christians to the point of public execution. After his dramatic conversion to faith in Jesus as the Messiah, Paul's academic training as a Pharisee was to become hugely beneficial to those seeking sound doctrinal anchors for this new expression of service to God. Saint Paul, in particular, accepted the concept that the sacrifice of Christ provided eternally what the sacrifice of a

Passover lamb had done each year. Thus, the absence of the temple and altar was not calamitous in that respect. There were no further annual sacrifices required to those who received salvation through the once-shed Blood of Christ crucified.

As evangelists travelled and debated as far afield as North Africa, eastwards into the subcontinent towards northern India, northwards into the Levant and around through Anatolia, and westwards across the Mediterranean regions of Europe, so converts were added to the Christian Faith whose backgrounds in culture and religion were diverse in the extreme. While sound apostolic teaching went a long way towards peaceful convergence in their newfound spiritual lives, friction between groups of Christians was inevitable.

Communications of the day were slow and relied heavily on travel routes providing safe passage for letters and messengers. The early concentration points of Christianity were in Jerusalem, Antioch, Rome, and Alexandria. There especially the leaders of Christians were tasked with teaching doctrine and religious expression in what we would refer to in modern corporate speak as 'silo type management organisation'. The most senior Bishop of each region would have had a lot of leeway and independence to lead and support local congregations, or *ecclesia*. They were primarily motivated to bring people to faith after all, and not to build a religious powerbase.

We read of a debate that threatened to prove fractious in Luke's book of the Acts of the Apostles, in chapter 15. The build-up of tension was caused by men who had travelled from Judea to Antioch, where they remonstrated with the local Christians, stating that circumcision was necessary for salvation. This had been a mark of divine covenant from the time of Abraham and had been included in Mosaic Law. The agitators from Judea insisted that this be considered as law for new converts from Gentile and Pagan backgrounds as well. Paul happened to be teaching in Antioch at the time and fiercely debated in disagreement. An ecclesiastical decision was made to send Paul and Barnabas to Jerusalem so that they could refer this matter to the apostles there. Once in Jerusalem and with the matter under consideration, Peter reminded all present that not even the most devout had ever been able to keep the burden of Mosaic law, and that *"...we believe that through the grace of the Lord Jesus Christ we shall be saved in the same manner as they"* (V11).

Saint James vocally agreed, adding that the new Christians, turning to faith in Jesus as Messiah as they were from many different backgrounds, should not be burdened with the full Mosaic Law – except for a short list of sin que non items. These instructions were that Christians should abstain from consuming food offered to idols, from consuming blood, consuming the meat of animals that had been strangled, and from sexual immorality. A divinely received concept is that the life of a being is in its blood. Old Testament laws forbade the consuming of lifeblood. Avoiding Pagan idol offerings speaks for itself, especially considering the subject we are dealing with here at large. Strangled animals will have lifeblood in them, so hence are forbidden.

The apostles and church elders sensed that they had received wisdom from the Holy Spirit, and so a letter was written to convey these as instructions, which was then delivered to the congregation in Antioch by Saint Paul and several other apostles.

The above events demonstrated to the new Christian converts that the Jewish traditions and manner of keeping religious observance were not passed on to all as rules for salvation. Certainly, those wishing to observe Passover could do so, but the legalism of Mosaic Law, in all its detail, was not required to be kept. What was required, very specifically, was to avoid idolatrous Paganism and all forms of immorality, especially in relation to one another.

Skipping forward in time to the fourth century Roman Catholic writer, Socrates Scholasticus, who wrote the *Ecclesiastical History Book V* (5). In chapter 22, a particularly long chapter in comparison to others in Book V, he affirms that neither the apostles nor the gospels impose the yoke of servitude on Christians to what were, at that time, considered to be Jewish rites. Let us be very clear here that we are considering observance of holy days of remembrance, and not moral laws, which should be followed whole-heartedly.

Scholasticus also considered those favouring the observance of Passover, who railed against Christians keeping any attention to Easter, to be unreasonable. This needs to be seen in the context of attitudes prevalent of the day. The majority of Christians – then under the protection of fellow Christian, Emperor Constantine – were, after many years of persecution by authorities, converted from Paganism and carried social inertia regarding festivals and celebrations. Many of the believers from the areas outside of the Middle East had no connection whatsoever to Jewish customs.

Scholasticus is described as being ambivalent regarding the details of holy days around Passover/Pascha, as long as they celebrated the memory of the 'saving passion'. The keeping of Passover itself was not regarded as law, nor was neglect penalised. Here you get an inkling of the diametrically different thinking in the Church at the time, and of the undercurrent of conflict between those with any say in church affairs.

These differences came to one of many breaking points during the fourth century because church leadership communicated more and more with central seats of authority, and so these details of divergence were highlighted in communications. Bishops from the regions around the Christian world did not always keep their expressions of opinion polite, and arguments became acrimonious. The leader over most of the Christian world at that time was Emperor Constantine. His father had been a Christian, and after Constantine observed the effectiveness with which Christians seemed to have in serving the God of the Christian Faith in comparison to his observations of Pagan followers at the time, he was persuaded to adopt the Christian Faith. From descriptions at the time, it seems that his faith was initially intuitive and academic as opposed to deeply spiritual, however, his life choices from then on indicate that he had made a firm commitment to faith as early as AD 1312.

Before Constantine battled and defeated Maxentius, the tyrant leader of Rome, he is recorded to have had a vision in which Christ appeared to him and showed him an image of a lighted crucifix-type image, with the exhortation, "By this, conquer". The cross became the standard under which his armies marched, and conquer they certainly did.

Constantine ruled as Emperor over many cultures and language groups. It was in the interest of unity to create conformities and standards that would guide all these various groups towards a workable common ground. The issues at stake were more than religious, but here we will cover just our subject matter.

A disagreement had arisen regarding calendar usage. This affected the realm at large, because joining the subjects under a common calendar and time reference would go a long way towards being able to manage so vast an empire. Power play was very much in the mix too, as there was a trend developing among centres of power to attempt to dictate local norms on neighbours, and so establish dominance. The Emperor would need to dominate proceedings in order to be a world authority.

During the preceding centuries, differences became apparent in how calendar dates were calculated. Some referred to the Jewish lunar calendar method of starting the new calendar year and thus setting days for Pascha. The 14th day of their month of Nisan was the day from which Pascha was deduced. Christians following this method were called Quartodeciman. The Church from Rome specified the first Friday after that 14th

Nisan as Good Friday, and would also add fuel to the Sunday Sabbath debate. Bishops in opposing camps tried to force the issue by excommunicating those espousing differing views, branding disagreement as heresy. Witness Bishop Victor of Rome excommunicating those following the Quartodeciman method, a judgement widely disputed and ignored by other Bishops.

In the year AD 325, Emperor Constantine convened an ecumenical council in order to settle the more fractious issues plaguing Church unity at the time. The Ecclesiastical History and writings of the historian Eusebius cover the proceedings and provide us with details. Even though we can expect historians to present a favourable image of an absolute ruler providing their patronage, it does appear to the reader that Emperor Constantine acted with great wisdom and cool judgement in managing these great debates between the luminaries of the Church. He went to much effort to calm tempers and encourage forgiveness and unity. Points of view were bounced around those ancient halls of power, tabling and settling disputes in turn.

Major uproar and disagreements were created by Paschists who wished to preserve parallels and continuity with Passover into the Christian age. These mostly represented those antecedents of the Eastern Orthodox sector. They also claimed that only the Jewish Sanhedrin should have the authority to determine the new moon year and festival times, which they had been doing until then. The Bishops in Jerusalem would obtain the dates from the Sanhedrin and then pass this information on to Christians in the area. In hearing the calendar usage issue and desiring to create synergy among those under his rulership, Constantine seems to have decided on the result based on majority rule, local tradition, and some anti-Semitic sentiment. He wanted to stamp his authority on proceedings and simultaneously prompt those around the far reaches of the empire to reference Constantinople for common timing and date setting. Rome was winning the old-world power struggle over Jerusalem, Antioch, and Alexandria.

Sunday Sabbath was another debate regarding time and date, which was settled at the Council of Nicaea. The Sunday Sabbath decision was partly taken in order to attract and keep Pagan follows to the faith. Later, after the Council of Laodicea, the Catholic Church enforced Sunday Sabbath on pains of excommunication.

A unifying expression of faith was written, debated, and fine-tuned. This we know today as the Nicene Creed. The wording of the creed was chosen in order to isolate and remove a heresy of the time, known as the Arian heresy. It had to do with the origin and substance of Jesus before His birth as a human on earth, and had caused consternation and no small degree of animosity between church leaders. The originator of this heresy was a man called Arius, who was excommunicated for his false teachings.

Once the council was concluded, over 300 Bishops and other church leaders returned to their congregations and parishes in every corner of the Empire, taking with them these newly promulgated unified standards of church norms. These became the founding principles on which evangelism and catechism were based for the foreseeable future of the faith. The mix of traditions, observances, and standards was carried forward into the wild frontiers of the Roman Empire. During the centuries that followed, we see the entrenchment of Easter traditions, especially within the European church, falling as they did under the influence of Rome.

CHAPTER 5

CHRISTIANISATION OF PAGAN EUROPE

Until the Great Schism of AD 1054, where the official separation between the Roman Catholic West and the Orthodox East occurred, the Church can be thought of as an entity mostly united in theology and effort. The Church grew by evangelism, teaching, example, and humanitarian outreach. Bishops in the major centres of the faith provided leadership to the priests and congregants under their pastoral care. Monasteries copied and preserved the Holy Scriptures, and Bible truths and Church traditions were taught to the young and new converts by catechism and from the pulpit.

As we remember from earlier chapters, the Pagan habits and traditions of the Mesopotamian region had spread into Europe many years prior to Christianity. Each of the tribes encountered by the Roman Empire during its conquest of Europe exhibited some form of Pagan observance, many with overlapping themes that included festivals aimed at venerating a goddess of fertility. While the local names and traditions differed, the common theme persisted across the continent. This was the belief system being encountered by most churchmen who forayed into what they considered the uncivilised hinterland.

We speak now of the Roman Catholic experience because we are considering how Christians came to mix Pagan practices with Christian calendar events, focusing on Europe. The Roman Catholic Church dominated the western regions of the continent, with the Orthodox Church gaining converts east and north of Constantinople. It would not be a stretch to imagine that the pioneers of the Orthodox Church encountered a strong Eostre tradition among their Pagan converts, especially in the regions of Mesopotamia where those practices had originated.

We have already seen how Scholasticus seemed ambivalent for his part about Christians celebrating their salvation on the dates associated until then with Easter. The Council of Nicaea also established the European calendar as the official date keeping method for the Empire under Constantine. Many aspects of Pagan life existed, firmly entrenched in the habit and mindset of the general population. Christian leaders and teachers were faced with seemingly insurmountable obstacles when endeavouring to pass on the Gospel of Christ in its pure simplicity. Pagan practices were so deeply entrenched in community and private life that a thorough re-education of the populace was required.

The first individuals of a community to accept salvation through Christ would have found themselves to be suddenly thrust into a position where their new beliefs and behavioural standards stood at odds to those of their past life; beliefs which were still held dear by the majority of their family and neighbours. Social and economic exclusion because of their new faith often followed, causing pain and suffering to the converts. Missing out on family and cultural gatherings is tough to deal with, especially when it is also required to explain these deprivations to children and close friends.

The chief reason for evangelism in Christianity is out of love for the eternal state of the souls of mankind. While individual churchmen would doubtless have been motivated by ulterior motives such as self-aggrandisement and building up a religious following, the purer drive to bring the light of salvation is a more plausible source of efforts made among the Pagan wildlings. The priority thus having been set; finer points of festival observance might easily have taken a back seat. If a new convert who truly accepted the Christian Faith, and who celebrated his or her salvation on a date set by a previously Pagan authority anyway, were to incorporate into this celebration symbols associated with Pagan fertility rites, then so be it for the time being. The parish priest could quite possibly have been a Pagan before his conversion, carrying the social norms of the day into his ecclesiastical work.

Cultural pressure was not the only reason for Pagan habits to persist. Education and literacy levels were low by modern standards. People obviously had common sense, wisdom, gifts of perception, and some individuals would have been enlightened through travel, but the availability and exchange of information was miniscule in comparison to today. Understanding among the laity was largely dependent on what was taught, sometimes dictated, from the lectern and pulpit. With a proverbial wall to climb in spreading the Gospel across Europe, priests and Bishops did not completely root out the inclusion of Pagan aspects from Christian observance. The Church, after all, had made concessions to accommodate Pagan conversions, including the adoption of the Sunday Sabbath and the dates for Easter as the Christian Pascha date.

Many in the Church have questioned the validity of conversions where the populace of a nation was influenced by the conversion of their leadership, usually a monarchy. The argument being that their Christianity was nominal at best, and did not entirely reflect each individual state of heart. There are points to be made for each argument, however, seeing that God can and does look at the heart and motives of an individual without hindrance, we should perhaps follow the scriptural injunction to judge not, except for judging ourselves.

The trend in European society was for the Gospel to be accepted more readily and earlier in urban areas with the agrarian countryside populations taking much longer to leave their traditions and adopt the Faith. Individuals from the more densely populated areas tended, on average, to have higher literacy rates and social sophistication. Once the town dwellers were established as Christians, parish churches became the focal point for gatherings when birth, marriage, and death occurred – the colloquial hatches, matches, and dispatches.

A pragmatic response from the Church to the co-existence of Pagan and Christian elements in society was gradually adopted. *Interpretatio Christiana* was the name given to the practice of converting native Pagan cultural aspects, imagery, sites, and calendar usage to Christian use. The Venerable Bede, great historian of the time, wrote in *Historia ecclesiastica gentis Anglorum*, of a letter from Pope Gregory I to Mellitus. In it he argues that conversions are made easier if people are allowed to retain the outward traditions but are taught to inwardly hold these symbols in honour of the grace of God. Keep the tradition but change the reason. For better or worse in terms of the problems that future generations of catechists would encounter when teaching truths to their pupils, this general attitude was adopted at the time.

Syncretism is the blending of different beliefs and practices where compatibility is assumed. There can be no assumption of compatibility between Christian and Pagan beliefs, however the concept of demonstrating new life and rejuvenation can be achieved by using similar symbols. Overlap was bound to occur, resulting in the acquiescence to some Pagan traditions by an overworked and endangered priesthood contending night and day for the Faith.

When contemplating the mixing of traditions, it is important to remember the timespan involved. One too easily overlooks the years, decades, and centuries that passed during the evangelisation of Europe at large. A procession of Popes, both good and bad, occupied the seat of Peter in Rome, who exerted varying degrees of influence over the catechism of the continents' faithful.

Let us look at some of the notable timestamps. Constantine I, then Emperor over a unified Roman Empire, arrived at a personal faith in Christ and soon afterwards made a firm commitment to apply the Apostolic and Scriptural tenets of the Christian Faith to how he ruled his empire. In AD 313 he issued the edict of Milan, which made Christianity legal in all of the Roman Empire. Armenia was a province of the Empire. A Christian called Saint Gregory the Enlightener brought the Gospel of Christ to the Armenian royal court after much persecution and imprisonment. Following the conversion of the Armenian king Tiridates the Great, the Christian Faith was proclaimed as the national religion, making Armenia the first country in the world to do so. The year was AD 314, just one year after the Edict of Milan made it possible to take that step without fear of sanction from Constantinople.

The use of Pagan temples, symbols, and also Pagan sacrifices were gradually abolished in the Roman Empire, including at the AD 392 Olympic Games. It was later Emperor Marcian who imposed the death penalty on anyone carrying out Pagan rites.

The Franks were the first Germanic tribe to accept the Christian Faith. This after their king, Clovis I, made the decision to convert in AD 496. The Lombards were to follow in the sixth century. During this time the continuation of Pagan symbology was widespread, observable in the artefacts and oral tradition surviving from these years. The rest of Europe heading westward, and northward from the Frankish territories was evangelised from the seventh to the fifteenth centuries. Charlemagne, later king of the Franks, triumphed in the Saxon wars, extending the regions in which the Christian Faith could be preached, shared, and lived out without oppression. Saint Patrick was of course the famous missionary to Ireland, becoming the patron saint of the Emerald Isle. He was a Romano-British Christian who was taken by an Irish raiding party in Roman Britain and was made a slave in Ireland. After escaping and making his way back home via France, Patrick heeded a vision of pleading Irish, and returned to lead the Pagan tribes there to faith in Christ.

Many interesting historical accounts exist of the acceptance of Christ as Lord in place of the Mesopotamian deities. The Slavic countries in central Europe mostly followed the pattern where the sequence of events began with the conversion of the reigning monarch, who then included the royal family, followed by the aristocracy and influential families in turn. Pagan symbols and traditions then began to wane in proportion to the importance attributed to their removal by those in authority. Some usage and tradition stubbornly remained.

CHAPTER 6

THE MODERN VIEW

Now that we have covered some details regarding the origin of the Christian Passover and how the observance has changed over the years, perhaps it would be instructive to include the points of view of the leadership of some Christian denominations. I was interested to hear from those putting sermons, liturgy, and children's teaching programmes together, just how much, if any, of the Pagan teachings continue to be perpetuated in modern churches. Using South Africa (my present home) as the place of reference, I approached the various Dioceses for input, and am sharing here their comments in as unedited a form as I can reproduce from conversations held.

The largest and among the oldest denomination is the Roman Catholic Church (RCC), often referred to simply as the Catholic Church. Bearing in mind that the word 'catholic' means universal, any church holding to the same confession is also catholic, but let's not split hairs. Their worldwide members number over 1.2 billion and are found in practically every country of the world.

Roman Catholic Paschal tradition expressed locally includes the use of decorated candles gilded with a cross, an alpha and omega, and the digits of the current calendar year written in the quarters made by the cross. The candles are lit by passing the flame from one to another, representing the witness of the light of Christ from one to another. Five grains of incense represent the five wounds of Christ on the Cross. Where adult baptism occurs, the Paschal Festival is a popular time for it to take place. The candle is called a Paschal candle, not an Easter candle. Mass takes place on Sunday morning; the candle lighting occurs after midnight from Saturday into Sunday. The local RCC congregations give some candies to the children after the Sunday service, however Easter symbols do not form part of the church or catechism activities, and there are no parallels drawn for the young linking the candy design with their faith.

The Anglican Church also enjoys a global presence. In the Anglican Communion there are 85 million people, and 25 million in the Church of England. In conversation with the leaders of various local chapels it was confirmed that Easter symbols do not form part of the liturgy or tradition. The church will have a sombre meeting on the Thursday evening, ending with the extinguishing of all lights, both electric and candles. The darkening of the church and the silence maintained by parishioners represent, with some emotional force, the death of Jesus, the apparent extinguishing of the Light of the World. Congregants silently file out of the church building in the dark, to return for an early service on Sunday. This sunrise service is the closest reference to Easter one can find. All readings and symbols are Christian in nature. The children are sometimes led in building an artistic model of a scene from the garden of Gethsemane, featuring an empty tomb and sometimes angels. This may be colloquially referred to as an Easter Garden, but the elements of the scene include only those found in the biblical account.

The Lutheran Church could be regarded as the oldest recognised protestant church. Worldwide they have 70 to 90 million members, depending on how affiliations are counted. They have a conservative order of service but do not display statues. Their Paschal service, readings, and traditions do not include any of the usual suspects of the Easter rites.

The Orthodox Church is another group that, as a whole, represents many millions of members. This includes 15 million in the Greek Orthodox Church alone. Russian / Eastern / Oriental followers number upwards of 150 million. Further groupings include the Coptic or Egyptian Church. The Coptic Orthodox Church is represented in Johannesburg by Bishop Antonius Markos, based at their church and seminary grounds in the suburb of Parkview. The Bishop was kind enough to spend some time explaining the various traditions and symbols used during their Paschal services. The Orthodox Church holds Pascha as the most holy observance and elevates the occasion above Christmas. Among other icons and symbols, they bake on site a special bread that is perforated to indicate the wounding of Christ as the bread of life. The bread is the flat bread variety of medium size, about an individual's portion. Members of the congregation prepare the breads, which are a firm favourite among those attending services. No quarter is given during official liturgy and teaching to the symbols of Easter.

Many freedoms are given to individual ministers across various denominations, but generally Easter traditions will only creep in during extra activities arranged by church members and not as part of the liturgy. This will be true across the gambit of denominations.

Messianic Jewish believers generally follow traditions passed down from biblical times, with differences in detail stemming from the long-term geographical and social separation between Sephardic and Ashkenazi communities. A Messianic Rabbinical Council offers easily researched advice to those wanting to keep observances in proper decorum. They are informed by the Mosaic Pentateuch (Talmud), the Tanakh (Old Testament), and the apostolic writings of the New Testament. Their advisories seem to be given in the spirit of 'we inform, you decide'. They seek to preserve the instructions of the Holy Scriptures, faithfully and appropriately expressed in modern society. The dates observed are those based on the lunar calendar for the 14th day of Nisan and forward. Symbols, service liturgy, and teachings are strictly scriptural. Here as well we find no inclusion of Pagan Easter tradition.

The same response regarding eschewing of Pagan symbols was received from all the church leaders whom I contacted with the question. In particular, the Baptist response was telling. The Baptist Church interior is usually kept visually plain and demure. Minimalist lines bordering on austerity are interrupted only by the occasional mural or cloth wall hanging depicting biblical motifs. Baptist interiors do not display the imagery and iconography so ingrained in the older denominations, the focus is on scripture and worship. Here the adult service and Sunday school for children place more focus on teaching content than on using symbols and images. While the use of Easter symbols is not overtly condemned, the focus remains on solid biblical teaching.

So, we see that the modern-day persistence of the Easter story and articles associated with the old Pagan rites originate from the secular world more than an uninformed Church. If anything, it is the laity who are not as informed as one would hope. Perhaps church teachings on what to avoid have proven unpopular, leading to hesitancy on the part of church leaders and pastors to address the issue of the inappropriate use of Pagan symbols among Christians during the Paschal days. Spare a thought for those responsible for shepherding a modern society so easily distracted. Restrictive teachings have become too unpopular for people to bear in the modern age, and sadly some in the church have adjusted their teaching content to accommodate public sensitivities.

One does understand the motive to maintain a positive message from pulpit and bulletin, however perhaps a balanced approach, gently taught, would be instructive without putting people off? Who would hazard a guess as to where the balance lies? If the search for Truth remains a strong human drive, individuals will continue to question the status quo and uncover what they are looking for. We are living in the information age after all.

CHAPTER 7

WHY DOES IT MATTER?

We are now familiar with the origins of many of the current symbols and traditions in use over the Paschal days. Considering that where we are today is a result of development over millennia, one could justifiably ask why any clarification, or adjustment in thinking, is required. If things have been going along swimmingly for centuries, barring some interdenominational battles and executions long ago, why is there any call to shine a light on inaccuracies? Surely we have inherited more than lies from our fathers?

I am sure that my fellows in the Christian Faith will be true to form in voicing opinions as diverse as one can imagine, however I would like to put forward a point of view that I believe keeps to the broad middle ground, and establishes a heartfelt motivation for disturbing the peace.

The crux of the matter is exactly that – the Cross, and what one believes about both Calvary and the empty tomb in Gethsemane. If the days of observance are just a long weekend for traditional holidays, then the traditions are malleable, and the symbols used are of no importance whatsoever.

Significance originates out of a genuine faith in the saving grace of Calvary, the hope of eternal life through the resurrection of Jesus Christ from death and hell, and His ascension to heaven and seating at the right Hand of God the Father. This observance of Pascha becomes elevated to be the central and pivotal annual event on the Christian calendar. Modern believers are unique in not keeping the Christian Passover as the pinnacle of festivals. Historically, all Church denominations held Pascha as the highest holy day of the year. Orthodox believers generally still do, and the Roman

Catholic Church still places much emphasis on the days. The mostly western protestant denominations have tended towards placing more emphasis on Christmas, in large part due to the pervasive consumerisation of that day by commercial interests representing every faith under the sun. The gaudy decorations appear in shopping malls as early as October, and vendors of every persuasion punt shiny trinkets, weak toys for the masses, and expensive luxuries that many can ill afford. As an aside, they are only successful insofar as one is willing to be swept along with the hype and hysteria.

The use of Pagan symbols and equivocation by early church fathers and teachers when explaining the Gospel story to Pagans during the early years of the spreading of Christianity has left a stubbornly resistant usage of the Pagans' Easter symbols in the Church. It is fun to hunt for chocolate eggs as a child, is there any wonder that the traditions would persist?

The turning motivation, at least as I see it, is that we are not illiterate, ancient, sun-worshipping Pagans. We don't need to be schooled as if we were children, nor be patronised by an autocratic church leader. We are blessed to live in the information age, where we have access by a multitude of avenues to comprehensive knowledge on practically any subject for which we have the time and inclination to research. False news and whacky conspiracy theories abound, but with multiple sources consulted – which include educated leaders from various church groups – one is able to, at length, filter out the static and arrive at a commonly held conclusion.

If we wish to, as the title says, purify our observance of this pivotal Christian celebration, we could make a case for replacing Pagan symbols with more demonstrably Christian options. Symbols aren't just empty things; they tell a story and carry meaning. That's why companies and creative types so carefully protect the reproduction and display of the symbols and designs that they produce. The trademark and related sections of the intellectual property industry and law are established for that very purpose. We wouldn't knowingly present ourselves with an incorrect symbol in public, anyone has that much sense. Imagine an extreme example such as wearing street gang colours in the opposite side of town, or a swastika to synagogue, or the brand of a competitor to one's place of employment. This is so self-evident that doing so could be expected only from the village idiot.

So why are we comfortable using borrowed Pagan symbols among our family for the pivotal event on the Christian calendar? Perhaps it boils down to knowledge and information. What you don't know can't disturb your peace. Once we do know, however, we are then faced with another of life's myriad choices. Not that the choice is binary, such as a requirement that puts one on a path to an eternal destiny, but hopefully this information prompts the will and desire to examine our choices from the heart.

In short, it should matter to us if the images we use to convey spiritual truths are accurate or not. These are the images that we imprint on the minds of our impressionable young children, which they carry with them each year during that time.

Referring first to the highest claim on our allegiance, let us see what, if anything, our Lord has to say on the matter. In the time since Noah, Pagans have been idolatrous. This was understood as a focus and worship of something other than the God who Noah confessed. Any of the immediate descendants of Noah who worshipped an idol knew full well that their attentions were misplaced. Later generations who were not under Noah's direct tutelage were perhaps less informed of their heritage, and hence easier to mislead with heretical teaching. Once Nimrod had established some human credibility by means of martial power, he and Semiramis carried enough social influence to establish idolatry as a common religious practice in their geographical area.

When the Lord detailed His requirements of the Israelites by giving them the Ten Commandments, among others, idolatry was specifically forbidden in the second commandment. No making of, bowing down to, or worshipping of any image is allowed by anyone professing Jehovah as God and Lord. Future generations would find themselves severely punished for breaking this rule. These instructions are reiterated in Deuteronomy 12:30, but does the Bible mention these specific forms of idolatry in a negative light? Good question. We find several references of God's displeasure at this expression of Paganism.

Reading in the book of Jeremiah 7:16-20:
" 'Therefore do not pray for this people, nor lift up a cry or prayer for them, nor make intercession to Me; for I will not hear you. Do you not see what they do in the cities of Judah and in the streets of Jerusalem? The children gather wood, the fathers kindle the fire, and the women knead dough, to make cakes for the queen of heaven; and they pour out drink offerings to other gods, that they may provoke Me to anger. Do they provoke Me to anger?' says the Lord. 'Do they not provoke themselves, to the shame of their own faces?'"

Therefore thus says the Lord God:
"Behold, My anger and My fury will be poured out on this place—on man and on beast, on the trees of the field and on the fruit of the ground. And it will burn and not be quenched."

These are not exactly the words of a proud parent, are they? The queen of heaven mentioned refers to Semiramis, and the cakes are the buns, erstwhile offerings to her – which later were redeemed when morphed into hot cross buns applying the principles of *Interpretatio Christiana* and Syncretism, covered in chapter five.

An incidence of stubborn continuation of idolatry by Israelites is found in Jeremiah 44:15-19, with ruinous consequences predicted in the passage which follows this one:

"Then all the men who knew that their wives had burnt incense to other gods, with all the women who stood by, a great multitude, and all the people who dwelt in the land of Egypt, in Pathros, answered Jeremiah, saying: 'As for the word that you have spoken to us in the Name of the Lord, we will not listen to you! But we will certainly do whatever has gone out of our own mouth, to burn incense to the queen of heaven and pour out drink offerings to her, as we have done, we and our fathers, our kings and our princes, in the cities of Judah and in the streets of Jerusalem. For then we had plenty of food, were well-off, and saw no trouble. But since we stopped burning incense to the queen of heaven and pouring out drink offerings to her, we have lacked everything and have been consumed by the sword and by famine.'

"The women also said, 'And when we burnt incense to the queen of heaven and poured out drink offerings to her, did we make cakes for her, to worship her, and pour out drink offerings to her without our husbands' permission?'"

The peoples' refusal to repent of idolatry resulted in a prophecy and fate for them that included destruction, famine, and deportment to foreign countries as indentured labourers.

In the book of Judges 10:6 onwards, we read an account of how divine protection over Israel was withdrawn because they worshipped the Baals and Ashtoreths, which we now know as Ashtur/Ishtur, the usual suspect. The neighbouring Philistines and Ammonites were able to defeat and oppress the Israelites until the Israelites communally repented of their idolatry, at which point a leader emerged who was able to wage a divinely-inspired battle plan against their enemies and escape from under their heel. The history of Israel reads like a see-saw of good versus bad practices by the Israelites. Negative consequences always followed after the people abandoned obedience to and service of God. The fallout after backslidden faith is metronomic in its predictability, borne out by historical record.

Ezekiel 8:13 onwards recount the Lord's displeasure at the people weeping for Tammuz and worshipping the sun, Pagan practices carried out in the Temple of Jerusalem. This was all in direct contravention of the first two commandments.

Okay, so that is clear enough from the Old Testament books. What about the New Testament, are there any references for us in the church age?

In 1 Corinthians 10:20-22 we are reminded that the gentile or Pagan sacrifices are made to demons, a situation in which a Christian should have no part. We aren't offering sacrifices when we have a Pagan Easter confectionery, but the point is that behind the innocent looking symbol lies a Pagan deity who would love to distract from and destroy any semblance of Christian Faith.

One should remember too that the book of Revelation details the eventual destruction of the mystery of Babylon, which includes any iteration that results from the departure from God at the time of Nimrod. This destruction of a mystery or hidden system will unfortunately take with it anyone clinging to it. The moral of the story is to not cling to things that represent an obvious departure from God's original intent for man. Once the truth behind Pagan symbols is learnt, why would an intentional Christian teach and share unsound practices with his or her kids?

CHAPTER 8

YOUR BEST CONCLUSION

If this book has been your introduction to the details of the crucifixion of Christ, or if you have seen a new angle to a well-known narrative, perhaps you are wondering that there seems to be a missing piece.

It is great that God made man for close and eternal relationship with Him, and also that after the fall of man and consequent separation from God, a system of forgiveness and reinstatement has been provided – first by an annual sacrificial lamb in the Jewish temple in Jerusalem, and then by the sacrifice of Jesus as the Lamb of God who takes away the sin of the world. What remains is to find out how to activate or receive that atoning forgiveness for ourselves as individuals. Be assured that God sees us all as individuals, created with freedom of choice. We will all be individually held accountable for whatever choices we make in life.

As we did earlier in the story, let us dispense – with any narrow denominational viewpoint, which all have merit, but might include centuries of human influence. What does God say through the writers of Scripture, about how man can be reinstated as righteous in God's sight, and be acceptable for entry into heaven after human death?

Before we get to the situation after Calvary, a short note on the time spent under the Mosaic Law is pertinent. Some may say that performance and obedience to the Law was how people became righteous and in good standing with God. Remember that the number of humans who have kept every law, and broken none, is zero. Every human who has ever lived has been imperfect and in need of cleansing in order to be able to relate to God. Human nature sees to that. So, even during the time covered by the Old Testament, people were saved by blood. The blood of the spotless lamb, to be exact. Today we are in equal need, as mentioned.

Jesus, when asked how man can be saved, said that one had to be born again. This He meant in a spiritual sense. Man's eternal essence is the spirit, it is what was made first during creation, the body came afterwards. We are a spirit, we have a soul comprising of our intellect, will, and emotional capacities. All these intangibles live in a body, the lowest form of our existence. Our spirit is also referred to in the Bible as the heart of mankind, denoting the spirit's place as the central core of man. You may have heard this spiritual rebirth being referred to by some denominations as giving your heart to Jesus to live in. It is in reference to the biblical analogy of the heart as the spirit or central essence of a person, and also to Jesus' description of how He and God (and the Holy Spirit) are one in the other with a person who accepts Jesus as the Messiah and their Lord.

We join this Holy family, are washed clean of sin, enter into eternal salvation, and begin a life in communion with God and fellow Christians by believing this in our hearts (and you know that means believing in your spiritual core) – saying with our mouths that we have sinned, need forgiveness, and accept Jesus as Saviour and Lord. This combination of confessing Christ is the origin of what is called a sinner's prayer, used to guide someone through a confession of coming to faith. I will include a prayer at the end so that anyone who would like to has a guiding format to use if you would like to commit your eternal Spirit to God. This is followed up by reading the Bible so that we can put God's Word / will into our minds, and whole-heartedly commit to changing our thoughts, motives, purposes, lifestyle, and actions to match up with the teachings we find there.

You might ask what happens if we fail? Do you mean *when* we fail? Confess to God, repent of evil, and believe that God is good to His Word that states that if we confess and repent of sin, He is righteous to forgive us our sin. Then forget the things of the past, and move forward in faith.

Here is a prayer of salvation:

"Heavenly Father, according to Your Word, I call on Your Name and on the Name of Jesus Christ, and I know that all those who call on Your Name shall be saved (Acts 2:21). I confess that I am a sinner, and that Jesus is the saving Christ. I believe in my heart that God raised Jesus from the dead, and so I receive salvation (Romans 10:9-10). I declare Jesus as the Saviour of my life. I also declare Jesus as the Lord of my life. I believe that the Holy Spirit makes His abode in my Spirit, and I commit to finding the will of God in His Word the Bible, and to living it out with God's help, for His glory."

If you prayed the prayer above in heartfelt earnestness, then you have been given the gift of repentance and have joined the Body of Christ. Join a Bible-teaching church, read a Bible every day, and pray whenever you have the opportunity. Join a community to be strengthened and to strengthen other brothers and sisters in the faith. God Bless!

BIBLIOGRAPHY

New King James Version of the Bible
American Catholic Quarterly Review, January 1883
Ecclesiastical History, Book V, Chapter 22, Socrates Scholasticus
Historia Ecclesiasticus Gentis Anglorum, Venerable Bede
The Case for the Resurrection, Lee Strobel
The Case for Easter, Lee Strobel
Christ in the Passover, Ceil & Moishe Rosen
Resurrection Witness, Doug Powel